Monsignor Knox discusses II Corinthians, xi. 18-21

"I think it's clear that among the other nasty things which had been said about St. Paul by his enemies, they had said he was always talking about himself, always trying to give a good account of himself. So he starts off, you see, 'Boast, do I? Well, what about these other people? . . . Look at the way they try to run the show at Corinth—won't let you call your souls your own!' What he's thinking of mostly, I fancy, is that other missionaries lived at the expense of the faithful, as they had a perfect right to do, but perhaps some of them lived a little too well at the expense of the faithful. St. Paul always made a point of carrying on his trade . . . so that there shouldn't have to be any second collection for the holy man's breakfast. . . . When he says, 'I speak as a fool,' that's what it means; he means 'this is a bit of vanity on my part.' "

ST. PAUL'S GOSPEL

by

RONALD KNOX

NEW YORK
SHEED & WARD
1950

NIHIL OBSTAT

Hugh F. Blunt, LL.D.
Censor Deputatus

IMPRIMATUR

✠Richard J. Cushing
Archbishop of Boston

Boston, November 8, 1950

MANUFACTURED IN THE UNITED STATES OF AMERICA

This series of Lenten Conferences was preached by Msgr. Ronald Knox in Westminster Cathedral on the Sunday evenings in Lent, 1950.

CONTENTS

THE PAULINE APPROACH

Our brother Paul, with the wisdom God has granted him, has written you a letter (II Peter iii. 15).

WHEN YOU have been looking at a child's picture-book, it may have occurred to you to wonder, before now, how the printer ever managed to transfer those brightly-coloured illustrations from the block to the paper. The process, of course, is not a simple one; in reality, there are three processes, and the page you are looking at has been three times through the press, receiving successively its tints of red, yellow and blue. So it is, if you come to think of it, about the knowledge you and I have of the basic facts of our religion; three different layers of evidence have been superimposed, one on the next. First, there is tradition. The earliest Christians learnt their faith by word of mouth; you and I, if God had so ordered our destiny, might still, after all these centuries, be learning our faith by word of mouth. Next, there are the holy gospels; an account of our Lord's life deliberately composed, for your information and mine, by men who had witnessed the events of it, or had lived so close to first-hand witnesses that the question of tradition hardly comes in. And finally, in the remaining books of the New Testament, you have a set of documents, mostly in the form of letters, written during the life-time of men who had seen our Lord. They don't set out to give us a course of religious instruction, but they are all the better as evidence for that. We learn from such writers in the course of conversation (as it were) how Christian people lived and thought in that first age, an age lit up by the afterglow of our Lord's own life on earth.

Leave out the four gospels, and most of the New Testament comes to us from the mind of one man, St Paul. I say 'from the mind' not 'from the hand,' because St Paul didn't usually write, he dictated. And you can trace his influence, no doubt, in the writings of other men who derived their inspiration from him. The Acts of the Apostles was written, not by St Paul, but by his friend St Luke; yet I think it is clear that St Paul must have encouraged him to write it, and supplied him with a good deal of his material. What shall we say of the Epistle to the Hebrews? The Church holds by the tradition that it was, in some sense, the work of St Paul, but the style of it differs noticeably from that of his acknowledged epistles. Must we suppose that, this time, he wrote with his own hand, wrote carefully, as a man writes when he is working out a thesis, instead of blurting out the thoughts of his pregnant mind, as he did to the stenographer? Or is it possible that he drew up a skeleton of the things he wanted said, and left some trusted disciple, Silvanus or another, to clothe it in his own words? Be that as it may, for our present purposes we will not use either the Acts of the Apostles or the Epistle to the Hebrews except here and there, by way of illustration. We will build up our picture of St Paul's gospel from those vivid, personal letters of his, thrown off in the heat of the moment to the Christians in Rome, Corinth, Galatia, Ephesus, Philippi, Colossae, Thessalonica, and to one or two of his immediate friends.

I want to study St Paul's letters in isolation, forgetting for the moment that we have any Christian tradition, any Gospel narrative, to supplement them. So, I imagine, you might get the printer to give you a pull-off of that childish picture all in blue, with the yellows and the reds left out. I want you to see what an admirable blue-print you can get, even so, of the Christian world-picture, simply from listening to what St Paul has to tell us. It is rather like listening to one side of a telephone conversation; we can only guess, as we go along, what the people at the other end of the wire have been saying. Our pattern will be all built up out of bits and pieces, just fragments of talk overheard, sparks struck from the anvil of forgotten controversies, and problems that have no meaning for us now. But we shall see, already, the outlines of our Christian world-picture etched in for us, and with a firm hand, by a man who is not thinking about us or our difficulties; he is just talking to his friends.

It is an extraordinary thing, if you come to think of it, how the account of our Lord which you get in the Gospels dovetails in with the account of him you get in the epistles. Not in the sense that the two accounts agree;

that would be natural, that would be commonplace; rather in the sense that they disagree. I don't mean that they contradict one another; I mean that the things on which St Paul concentrates his attention are things upon which, apparently, the Evangelists do not concentrate attention, and vice versa. After all, ask anybody in the world who has heard of Jesus Christ to tell you what kind of Man he was. You will be told, at once, that Jesus Christ went about the world doing good, healing the sick, giving sight to the blind, and so on. There is no word of that in St Paul; with him, the whole of our Lord's earthly biography passes unnoticed. Watch him, for example, when he is recommending to the Philippians the virtue of humility (Phil. ii. 5 *sqq.*). You would expect him to remind them how our Lord was born in a stable, his Mother a peasant; how he lived as a poor man, how he died as a common criminal. But it isn't, you find, our Lord's behaviour as Man that he appeals to for his illustration; it is the condescension of our Lord in becoming Man at all. Always he misses the opportunity of telling us a story, the story of the greatest Man who ever lived.

Again, think how much space is occupied in all the Gospels by long extracts from what our Lord said. Very probably, even before the Gospels were written, there were collections of such sayings handed on to the faithful by word of mouth. How often does St Paul quote the words of his Master? In the epistles, never*; only once in

* Except incidentally, when he describes the institution of the Holy Eucharist in I Cor. XI. 24, 25.

own life, but with his life, who died for us and has risen again. And therefore, henceforward, we do not think of anybody in a merely human fashion; even if we used to think of Christ in a human fashion, we do so no longer. It follows, in fact, that when a man has become a new creature in Christ, his old life has disappeared, everything has become new about him.' The interpretation of that passage is neither easy nor certain, but I think the kind of meaning St Paul means is this. It is for the beginner, for the man who is still finding his way into the Church, to study the proofs of our Lord's Divine mission, the miracles, the fulfilments of prophecy; it is for the beginner to learn by heart, if he will, our Lord's recorded sayings. But all that is to know Christ after a human fashion, to treat him as a Man who once lived but now is dead, the subject of a biography. Once you have learned to accept Christ, and to be united with him by baptism, everything becomes different; he who was once a dead Hero is now a living Friend. Difficult for us, after all these centuries, to think in those terms; we have to treasure up the least crumbs of information we can get about Jesus of Nazareth–it all happened so long ago. But in St Paul's time it was different; the Ascension had only happened the other day; the airs of grace were all about you; why should you go back over the past?

Some instinct of that kind it must have been, I think, which made St Paul and the other New Testament writers strike out a line for themselves, instead of constantly quoting our Lord, constantly appealing to his example, as we should have expected them to do. The Evangelists, you see, were so very much on their good behaviour; they were determined to tell a plain story, not dotting the I's or crossing the T's, leaving it to the reader to form his own conclusions. Every scene must be described just as it appeared to the people who saw it happen; there was to be no improving the occasion, no morals drawn, no theological footnotes. Their readers were to see the Hero of the gospels as a Man among other men, who lived and died at a given moment in history. All that he was, but for St Paul that was not the point. The point was that our Lord was alive; that he lived on in his mystical Body, the Church. When they met on the road to Damascus, our Lord said, 'Why dost thou persecute me?' and that ME remained in St Paul's thought as the keynote of all his theology.

No, they were not to think of Christ after a human fashion. His nature was Divine; if all things came from the eternal Father, they came from him through Christ; and that 'through' denoted, not a less ultimate responsibility, but somehow a more intimate relation. He was the Elder Brother of all created things, and it was suitable that when God determined to reconcile his rebel world to himself, Christ should be the focus in which all creation should be at once resumed and renewed. His nature was Divine, but the incommunicable privileges of Godhead were not allowed to detain him (Phil. ii. 6); somehow, he took upon himself the nature of Man, accepted all its inadequacies, shouldered all its responsibilities. He, our Elder Brother, our Representative, became our Victim, the Representative of our sin; hung upon the Cross, and, as if by the shock of that unparalleled encounter, shattered all the barriers that had existed till then (Eph. ii. 15) —the barrier between God and Man, the barrier between life and death, the barrier between Jew and Gentile. He died, and in his death mankind, as mystically associated with him, died too, so that the old debt incurred by Adam's sin was cancelled (Rom. vi. 6). He rose again, and thereby acquired a second title to the headship of the human race; he was the Elder Brother of all risen men (Col. i. 18). The life into which he rose was not a force that quickened his natural body merely; it quickened to birth a new, mystical body of his, the Church. In the power of that life the individual Christian becomes supernaturally alive; dead to sin, dead to the fetters of the old legal observance, he lives now in Christ, lives to God (Rom. vi. 10). Baptism, his initiation into his Master's death and Resurrection, leaves him, as it were, tongue-tied and gasping for breath, while the Holy Spirit within him cries out, 'Father, Father,' to claim the promise of adoption (Gal. iv. 6). Meanwhile, the Church as a whole is Christ's building, in which we all inhere, is Christ's Bride, inspiring and prescribing sanctity, is Christ's Body, of which we are cells. Our whole life now is Christ-conditioned, he is the medium in which we exist, the air we breathe; all our nature is summed up, all our activities are given supernatural play, in him.

That is St Paul's programme; and perhaps it is not to be wondered at if he passes over in silence the details of a biography, whose total effect so reverberates with theological significance. The Incarnation, for St Paul, did not mean primarily that God had become *a* Man; it meant primarily that God had become *Man,* had infected the human race, as it were, with his Divinity. 'The Life of Christ' is a phrase which suggests to you and me a book on a shelf, a book by Père Didon or Archbishop Goodier. For St Paul, the phrase had no such meaning; or anyhow, that was not the meaning which leaped to the mind. The Life of Christ was to him an energy that radiated all about him, was the very breath he drew in with his lungs.

Do you know what it is to meet some great man, or even some interesting personality that arrests you, and to go away quite forgetting how he was dressed or even what he looked like, because the inspiration of what he was saying riveted you at the time, so that you were unconscious of anything else? And afterwards, even what he said hardly remains in the memory; what exactly *did* he say? All you know is that a kind of glow pervades you, a kind of clarity that reveals your own thoughts to you, as the result of what passed. It is the man's personality that haunts you, something too subtle and too elusive to admit of analysis, something beyond the play of features or the sound of speech; the man himself has cast a kind of spell on you. Something like that happened to St Paul, I suppose, but in an infinitely higher degree, after his experience on the road to Damascus. The shock passed off, the blindness was cured; but always the interior sight of the apostle was dazzled by the memory of that interview. Stories about Christ, things Christ said, repeat them by all means, but St Paul wanted something more than that; he wanted Christ.

St Ignatius put it on record, that even if no documents of the Christian religion remained, he would have been prepared to die for the faith, in the light of what our Lord had made known to him at Manresa. And St Paul was in the same category.

There is, I think, something Providential about this attitude of the New Testament writers. Because St Paul contrives to fill in for us, like the blue plate which the printer superimposes on the red, our picture of what our Lord was like. I think there is, about the Synoptic gospels, a kind of deliberate objectiveness which sometimes makes it hard to understand the way in which their story develops. Why did the Apostles leave their nets and start out without a word, when our Lord said 'Follow me'? What was the magic of voice or look that drew them away, in those early days when no miracles had yet been done, when the campaign of preaching had not yet been opened? Something escapes us in their narrative; what we call, in the loose sense, 'personality'. The tremendous impact which his force of character made on people—do you remember how, according to St John, his captors in the garden went back and fell to the ground when he said, 'I am Jesus of Nazareth'? All that is difficult to realize in the Synoptist account. It becomes easier to realize when you watch the effect it had on St Paul; how, after that interview on the Damascus road, he saw Christ in everyone, Christ in everything; nothing but Christ.

Meanwhile, let us not be betrayed, even for one unguarded moment, into suggesting that St Paul's gospel was different from anybody else's gospel. There was no imputation which he would have met with a more vigorous protest; that we know, because the imputation was in fact made by rival teachers in his own day, anxious to undermine his influence. Always he describes his teaching as a tradition, something which he is handing on; beset with missionary problems, he will yet find time, not once or twice, to go back to Jerusalem and confer with those who were Apostles before him; 'Was it possible,' he asks, 'that the course I had taken was useless?' (Gal. ii. 2). No, we shall hear nothing from St Paul that is not in accord with the full stream of Christian theology. Only Divine truth is rich enough to admit of different angles of human approach. Grace does not destroy nature, it perfects nature; something of the human genius remains, and the pure gold of revelation is not always minted in the same work-shop. And St Paul's was no ordinary mind; sensitive, yet fearless, logical, yet poetic, infinitely tender with the scruples of others, yet unflinching in its honesty. A delicate instrument, it will interpret the melody of Christian thought in its own way. We must listen patiently, allowing him his own choice of language, not trying to fix on his words a meaning which has since become technical, not allowing our minds to be disturbed by the echoes of later controversy. You must come to St Paul with fresh eyes if you are to feel his magic.

ST PAUL AND THE OLD TESTAMENT

All that is an allegory. The two women stand for the two dispensations; Agar stands for the old dispensation, which brings up children to bondage, the dispensation which comes to us from mount Sinai (Gal. iv. 24).

EVERY YEAR, on the fourth Sunday of Lent, the epistle at Mass consists of an elaborate allegory, in which St Paul contrasts Sara with Agar, Isaac with Ismael, something (it is not clear what) with mount Sinai, and the earthly with the heavenly Jerusalem. Every year, the faithful listen with an air of polite detachment, evidently feeling that they cannot be expected to understand what all this is about. It is this business of the overheard telephone conversation once more; the Galatians, no doubt, had a clue to St Paul's meaning which we haven't. . . . Yes, but, before you say that, think. Who were the Galatians? Heathens quite recently converted; it was only a year or two, perhaps only a month or two, since they had mistaken St Barnabas for Jupiter, and St Paul for Mercury. Now, Jewish missionaries were trying to persuade them that, in order to be good Christians, they must adopt the law of Moses. What an extraordinary thing that these people, quite stupid country people, Gentile by birth, heathen by education, should be expected to know all about Agar, all about mount Sinai, and not only to know about them, but to understand the mystical significance of them, when you and I can't make head or tail of it!

There is only one possible explanation of it; and that is that St Paul, when he instructed enquirers in the faith, told them a great deal about the Old Testament, or at least about the books of Genesis and Exodus. Even if they were Gentiles, to whom the sacred books of the Jews meant nothing, they had got to learn about the Old Dispensation first, before they could see the New Dispensation in its right context, against its right background. Poor stupid slaves from Galatia had got to be taken all through the family history of Abraham and the patriarchs before they got on to the part about Jesus Christ. That is perhaps why, in writing to these same Galatians, St Paul refers to the ordinances of the Jewish law as 'those old schoolroom tasks' (Gal. iv. 9) ; the Jewish background of the Christian revelation is something that must be laboriously learnt, like the Gender Rhymes, like the Rule of Three; it is a preliminary grind which you have got to get through before your education proper really begins. It might seem dull, but there was no help for it; you must be properly grounded before you could master your subject, and the groundwork of the Christian religion was the story of the Old Testament, which the poor Gentiles had never heard of.

How then does St Paul look back on it, the panorama

of history, and the pattern which his own race had woven through it? As a mirror, I think, which reflects the mysteries of the New Dispensation, but reflects them, you might almost say, back to front. Most of us, when we were younger, have tried to cheat the hours of some long railway journey by kneeling up on the seat and watching the scenery flash past, telegraph poles and fields and distant hills, in the looking-glass. Then, when you had got thoroughly accustomed to the rhythm of its movement, you would turn round suddenly and look out of the window at the real scenery, flashing past in the opposite direction. St Paul's view of history is rather like that; he looks back over history and sees the world not merely as bad but as going from bad to worse; that terrible passage in the first chapter of the Romans is meant, evidently, to be a picture of contemporary manners. And the coming of Christ meant, for him, that all that process had gone into reverse; with the coming of Christ, history was repeating itself, but repeating itself just the other way round.

He saw our Lord as the second Adam, the Adam who rose, the Adam who restored us, as contrasted with the Adam who fell, the Adam who ruined us. A familiar consideration; but how many times is it mentioned in the Gospels? There is no allusion, from end to end of the Gospels, to the Fall of Man. Adam is only twice mentioned in the New Testament, outside St Paul's epistles, and both times merely in passing. How much St Paul was following the lines of current Jewish interpretation, when he laid such stress on the Fall, we cannot be certain; but the references to it in the Old Testament, outside the second chapter of Genesis, are meagre and inconclusive. The tradition of the Church would beyond doubt have preserved for us, in any case, the doctrine of the Fall, and some account of how it dovetails in with the doctrine of our Redemption. But, so far as Scripture is concerned, you may say it was St Paul alone, under the prompting of the Holy Spirit, who gave the Fall of Adam the place it has in Christian theology.

St Paul saw the Old and New Testaments as a series of parallel columns; he tells us as much in that passage from the Galatians which I gave you as my text. And the list begins quite simply, 'Adam equals Christ'. We must see Adam as the head of the human race by physical descent, as summing up in his own person the whole experience of humanity; then we shall begin to understand how Christ is the head of the human race by spiritual adoption, and how he sums up in his own person the whole experience of his Church. Because Adam was the head of the human race, the guilt of his transgression transferred itself automatically to his descendants. Oh, no doubt they were sinners too; nobody was more certain than St Paul about the corruption of heathen humanity. But he does not think of them, in this connexion, as imitating and therefore sharing the sin of Adam. He is speaking of transgression; and where there is transgression, there must be a direct commandment to transgress; after the Fall, until the law of Moses came, there was no such direct law issued to mankind, and yet mankind had to bear Adam's punishment. Death reigned; physical death, at once the symbol and the sequel of spiritual inanition. The status of guilt incurred by Adam's transgression lived on in us, his descendants in the natural order (Rom. v. 12–14).

The obverse of that medal is not difficult to read. Sprung from Adam by physical descent, we acquire the status of guilty men; incorporated into Christ by spiritual adoption, we acquire the status of men reprieved; that is what it means, to be justified. And as it is not, primarily, anything we do that makes guilty men of us, but mere birth from Adam, so it is not anything we do that justifies us, but mere re-birth in Christ. To become the second Adam, it was only necessary for our Lord to come to earth as Man; he 'took birth from a woman, so as to make us sons by adoption' (Gal. iv. 4). It is in that sense, probably, that we should understand an obscure passage in the first epistle to Timothy, where St Paul, after alluding to the sin of Eve, tells us that 'woman will find her salvation in the child-bearing' (I Tim. ii. 15); almost certainly, our Lady's Child-bearing is meant. More commonly, it is our Lord's Death and Resurrection that are represented as the gate of the new life which comes to us; mystically associated with our Lord, we die with him and rise again with him. But always St Paul will keep to his chosen symbolism; baptism does not remind him, as it reminds St Peter, of Noe coming out of his ark to repeople the world, does not chiefly remind him, as it reminds the Church on Holy Saturday, of Moses crossing the Red Sea at the head of a redeemed people. No, mankind begins with Adam, who became, as Scripture tells us, a living soul; it is fulfilled in the Adam who has become a life-giving spirit. In a garden the second Adam, like the first, awakes to life.

Meanwhile, there is a gulf of history to be bridged, between man's fall and man's redemption. Something, surely, happened, something of far-reaching importance to mankind, when God gave his law to Moses on mount Sinai. We are accustomed to think of mount Sinai as a partial revelation, and perhaps St Paul might have used the same language; 'the Jews' he writes 'had the words of God entrusted to them' (Rom. iii. 2) although it is doubtful whether 'promises' would not be a better rendering than 'words'. But St Paul thinks in terms of redemption, not of revelation; and where redemption is concerned he will not allow the Mosaic covenant even the dignity of a half-way house. Ever since Adam's fall, the ambition of Man was to be justified; that is, to get rid of the sentence of outlawry imposed on him, and to be once more what Adam had been, a *persona grata* with God. Towards the achieving of that ambition, the law of Moses has not brought us one step nearer; not a single step.

No, if anything the law left us worse off than we were before. 'It was brought in,' St Paul tells the Galatians, 'to make room for transgression' (Gal. iii. 19). What does that mean? Why, surely this; that the sins committed between the time of Adam and the time of Moses were not, strictly speaking, transgressions, because (as we have seen) there was no direct law to transgress. With Moses, God's law was expressly promulgated to mankind, and every sin after that was a transgression; nobody could plead that he didn't know he was doing wrong, because here was God's law in black and white to tell him that he was doing wrong. God's purpose, as always, was beneficent; by thus throwing our sins into relief, he made us more eager than ever for the coming of our redemption. But the Law didn't help us to get nearer to God, because we all immediately started disobeying it, just as if it wasn't there. The Psalm describes Almighty God as looking down from heaven to see if he could find a single innocent man; but no, there is nobody who reflects, and searches for God, all alike are on the wrong course (Rom. iii. 11; Ps. xiii. 2)—it was a moral which you could illustrate abundantly, at every period, from the writings of the prophets. The Jews, who had received the law, were nevertheless continually disobeying it. That means, evidently, that the law shewed us what was the right thing to do, without bringing us the grace which would enable us to do it; revelation without illumination. To prove his point, St Paul gives you in the Romans that terrible chapter which describes the soul, unbefriended by grace, seeing at every turn what is the right thing to do, and doing just the opposite. 'The sense of sin, with the law's ban for its foot-hold, caught me unawares, and by that means killed me. . . . It is

What, then, was God's solemn covenant with man? The promise made, long before, to Abraham. The prophets, when they appealed to the Divine fidelity, rested their claim chiefly on the promises made to king David; you will only find Abraham mentioned about seven times in the whole of their writings. But the older tradition survived; both in the Magnificat and in the Benedictus Abraham is the name of destiny. A series of prophecies had been made to him, of which the most far-reaching was, that in his posterity all the nations of the world should find a blessing. We must not lay too much stress on the actual form of the words. To say that all mankind will bless themselves in the name of Abraham's posterity does not mean more, necessarily, than that it will be used in formulas of benediction; 'May the Lord bless thee as he blessed the seed of Abraham'. But it was the tradition of the race that a more solemn assurance was involved; the remote issue of a homeless desert chief was, somehow, to acquire a world-significance. And had it, St Paul asks (Rom. iv. 14)? For a time it might have seemed as if the promise were being fulfilled, when Solomon's empire bridged the land-passage between east and west, receiving in its coffers the tribute of east and west alike. But all that was a thing of the remote past; the balance of the world had shifted, empires had changed hands, and the Jewish race was a despised, a scattered minority of mankind.

And now, with a stroke of the pen, St Paul sweeps away the whole edifice of Jewish privilege. Abraham believed God, and it was reckoned virtue in him; when was that? Before any law had been promulgated on Sinai, before the rite of circumcision had been enjoined, before the birth, even, of Isaac (Rom. iv. 10). It follows that the true descendants of Abraham are not those who claim his physical parentage, but those who share his faith. Carrying the war into the enemy's country, St Paul goes back to Ismael, the eldest son of Abraham, but born out of wedlock. And he allegorizes the whole story; Ismael, the natural son, serves for a type of physical descent, of outward observance, of the old covenant generally; Isaac, the child of promise, stands for a type of spiritual sonship, of interior religion, of the new covenant which was given to us in Jesus Christ (Gal. iv. 21 *sqq.*). St Paul has told us elsewhere that what is first in order of importance comes last in order of time (I Cor. xv. 46); man's body is created first, his soul afterwards. So it is here; Isaac, the late-born, who is despised by Ismael, and is none the less Abraham's heir—we are to see, in him, the image of the Christian Church, later in time than the synagogue, derided by the synagogue, and yet the final repository of God's mercies, the true explanation of his mysterious dealings with mankind, all those centuries ago.

And then, as if the lesson hadn't been made plain enough, the same situation repeats itself in Isaac's family as in Abraham's. Two brothers again; both, this time, born in wedlock; but Esau is the elder, Esau is his father's favourite. Esau is the world's choice, and Esau is rejected. How the Jews had relished that story, contrasting their own future greatness with the rude barbarism of their desert neighbours, the Edomites! But no, says St Paul, the contrast foreshadowed in the book of Genesis was not a contrast between two rival nations, both descended from Isaac. It was a contrast between two orders, the natural and the spiritual order; between those older things, the law of Moses, the pride of the Jews in their ancestry, and the newer thing that had come to pass, the birth of the Christian Church. Physically descended from Jacob, the Jewish people, like Esau, were being excluded from the promise of Divine mercy—or say, rather, they were excluding themselves from it, by their obstinate rejection of Christ (Rom. ix. 9 *sqq.*). Useless to ask, why God should allow such blindness to fall on them; you might as well ask why he allowed Pharaoh to harden his heart—indispensable prelude to the triumph of the Exodus. It is a mistake to read that ninth chapter of the Romans as if it were an essay on predestination and free will. St Paul is not thinking about all that; he is thinking about the rejection of the Jews, his fellow countrymen, so melancholy to witness, so difficult to understand (Rom. ix. 14 *sqq.*).

Always it is like that with St Paul; you cannot make any allusion to the Old Testament without his transposing it into a fresh key, restating it in terms of the New. Even the sins of Israel in the desert were recorded, he says, as a warning to us; to us, in whom history has reached its fulfilment (I Cor. x. 1 *sqq.*). Not a mirage,

ST PAUL AND CHRIST'S DIVINITY

He is the true likeness of the God we cannot see; his is that first birth which precedes every act of creation (Col. i. 15).

WHEN A MAN gets hold of a new idea, or rather, is got hold of by a new idea, which throws him off his balance and reinterprets the world for him, it may have any one of three effects on his daily conversation, and on his published writings. He may keep silent about it, except when he is in specially congenial company; he may have the feeling that this idea is so much too big for him, he will only spoil it if he tries to put it into his own words; people will take it up wrong, and be offended by it, or people will misunderstand it, and exaggerate it, and vulgarize it; far best, when the general public is listening, to hush it up. Or the effect may be just the opposite; he may be so full of his subject that he cannot resist bringing it up on any and every occasion; always he is wanting to buttonhole people and tell them about it, argue about it. Or, finally, it may become, from the first, part of the background of his mind, something which he takes for granted, and takes it for granted that everybody else takes it for granted too. He does not drag it in, does not harp on it, it seems to crop up naturally; it makes itself known in casual allusions, in the unconscious overtones of his thought. Now, which of those three effects did his conversion have on St Paul?

Rather unexpectedly, neither the first nor the second, but the third. The more you read his epistles, the more (I think) you get the impression that the mysteries of Christian theology are neither a difficult topic which he is anxious to avoid, nor the professed subject of his teaching, but his whole mental background, which keeps on shewing whether he means it to or not.

It would have been so easy to understand, if St Paul, writing when he did, writing for the sort of people who were going to hear his letters read out, had felt inclined to soft-pedal the note of dogma. After all, who were these people? Mostly, you would imagine, rather stupid people, many of them slaves, nearly all of them pagans till yesterday. As pagans, they had worshipped a whole pantheon; it had been hard enough to make them believe there was only one God—wouldn't the doctrine of the Trinity be rather confusing to them? As pagans, they had offered incense to the memory of dead emperors, deified now, the neuropath Tiberius, the madman Caligula—would they be able to see the point of the Incarnation? Wouldn't it be safer to tell them stories about the life of Jesus? But no, St Paul would spare them nothing. Contrariwise, if you *were* going to mention dogma, you would be inclined to rub it in, with a lot of simplification and a lot of repetition: 'Remember, three Persons, the Father, the Son, and the Holy Ghost'—staccato echoes of the class-room. But no, that is not St Paul's method either. He treats his converts as if they had been instructed as well as you or I—better than some of us; he will refer to the august mysteries of the Faith in an almost casual way; as if everybody, naturally, would understand all about *that;* he alludes to these things not because the guttersnipes of Philippi will need to be told about them, but because they happen, for the moment, to throw light on his argument; a mere reference, a mere allusion, and he passes on to something else. How strange it seems to us! And perhaps rather humiliating.

The doctrine of the Trinity—how little your attention is drawn to it as you read through the first three gospels! Only at the last moment, when our Lord is making ready to ascend into heaven, does he explain to his apostles that they are to baptize in the name of the Father and of the Son and of the Holy Ghost. With St Paul it is quite otherwise; he doesn't insist on the doctrine, but it keeps on cropping up. It's not merely that he closes an epistle with a formula of blessing which includes the threefold invocation (II Cor. xiii. 13). What is much more significant is the way his thought travels back, unbidden, to the subject we half expected him to avoid. He is telling the Corinthians that they ought not to quarrel about the importance of this or that spiritual endowment; after all, he says, all alike are the gift of the same Spirit. And then he adds, quite unnecessarily as it seems, 'just as there are different kinds of service, but it is the same Lord we serve, and different manifestations of power, though it is the same God who manifested his power everywhere in all of us' (I Cor. xii. 4, 5). He is not out to tell us anything about the Trinity, you see, but there is a kind of Trinitarian groove in his mind which carries it on from one Divine Person to another.

So it is when he has been talking to the Romans about the call of the Gentiles; he breaks out into praise of God's inscrutable wisdom, and once again there must be a threefold division; 'All things find in him their origin, their impulse, and their goal' (Rom. xi. 36). All things come *from* him; that is the turn of phrase St Paul regularly uses for God the Father. All things come *through* him; that is the turn of phrase St Paul regularly uses for the Divine Word. All things aspire *to* him; that is less natural and more difficult. But I think St Paul sees creation as an outward echo of that Divine Life which is shared by the three Persons of the Trinity. The Holy Spirit is that Love by which the cycle of the Divine Life returns upon itself; and the love which goes back to God from his creatures is therefore, as it were, his province; not because it is specially directed to him, but because he inspires and energizes it.

So it is again when St Paul is trying to promote a spirit of unity among his converts at Ephesus. You are one body, he writes, with a single Spirit, each of you, when he was called, called in a single hope; and then, after this threefold appeal to the Holy Spirit, there must be a threefold appeal to the Second Person of the Trinity, 'with the same Lord, the same faith, the same baptism'. And next, there ought to be a threefold appeal to God the Father; only St Paul is carried away, poetry as so often getting the better of logic, and finishes up with a fresh Trinitarian formula: 'who is above all, pervades all, and lives in all' (Eph. iv. 4 *sqq.*). This time, we will not examine his choice of words; spend too much attention on the details of what St Paul says, and you get left behind; the majestic sweep of his argument has passed you by. Enough to have satisfied ourselves that the doctrine of the Blessed Trinity is always close to the surface of St Paul's thought. If for no other reason, because that is the starting-point from which he approaches the doctrine of the Incarnation.

I said just now that we are to think of God's creation as an echo, an extension (if that word may be cautiously used) of his own Divine Life. The eternal act of generation by which the Father begets the Divine Word is the model and as it were the impetus of that external activity by which he creates things outside himself. And so, even before we have begun to talk about the Incarnation at all, it is natural for us to think of the Divine Word as in some sense the medium by which we approach the Godhead. 'For us,' St Paul says, 'there is only one God, the Father who is the origin of all things, and the end of our being; only one Lord, Jesus Christ, the creator of all things, and our way to him' (I Cor. viii. 6). In the same sense, the epistle to the Hebrews tells us that it was through his Son God created this world of time; 'without him' adds St John 'nothing came that has come to be'.

Somehow, by some title we cannot hope to understand, the Divine Word is to be thought of as the link between God and his creatures.

That notion St Paul has worked out for us in one passage which startles us by its richness and firmness of expression; will startle us still more if we remember that the Christian religion was only about thirty years old—how rapidly its thought had crystallized! St Paul is writing to the Church at Colossae, threatened with an invasion of that heresy which afterwards gave the Church so much trouble under the name of Gnosticism. The starting-point of the Gnostic is this: The world we see about us is such a hotch-potch of good and evil, you cannot possibly attribute the creation of it to one God, and a God who is infinitely good. No, you can only account for the facts by supposing that a whole unseen world of angels exists, much higher than ourselves but not enjoying the perfections of Divine Wisdom; between them, as the resultant of ill-balanced forces, these must have produced the world as we know it. Easy to see that such a doctrine did not look altogether unlike Christian doctrine; easy to see that it had attractions for the mind of a Christian who, till yesterday, had worshipped a whole multitude of gods. In recalling the Colossians to the right tradition of theology, St Paul is concerned to point out that no responsibility for the act of creation can rest with any Being outside the Godhead itself. Angels and men and all the rest of creation are the direct work of God, and in some special sense of the Divine Word.

Among all the short-comings of the Gnostic system this especially challenges his attention; it denies the unique position of the Second Person of the Blessed Trinity as the sole intermediary between things human and things divine.

With that in view, St Paul gives us a well-known description of the Son of God, as he exists independently of his human nature, independently of the work of redemption. 'He is the true likeness of the God we cannot see; his is that first birth which precedes every act of creation. Yes, in him all created things took their being, heavenly and earthly, visible and invisible; what are thrones and dominions, what are princedoms and powers? They were all created in him and for him; he takes precedency of all, and in him all subsist' (Col. i. 15). He is the true likeness of the God we cannot see—the Epistle to the Hebrews puts that in another way by saying that he is 'the radiance of his Father's splendour, and the full expression of his being' (Heb. i. 3). Perhaps the least misleading of all the images by which we try to understand the Divine Nature is that of the artist. Every artist will tell you that he is trying to express himself, yet when he has done his best he will acknowledge that he has failed; he did not express himself fully. He tried to put himself into his work, but only a little of it, he feels, is really there. But God the Father, in the eternal generation of his Son, does express himself fully; for once, the likeness is adequate to the original, and is one with it. Of that eternal act, the creation of all things visible and invisible is only a kind of echo, only a kind of ripple; but to that tenuous extent it reflects the Divine Paternity. That is why, St Paul tells us, creation stands in a special relation, or rather in a special series of relations, to the eternal Son of God. It comes to be *through* him; he communicates to it the impulse which gives it birth. It exists *in* him; he is the medium which gives it coherency. It exists *for* him; he is the end towards which all its imperfect efforts aspire. He is, in a sense, the elder Brother of every created thing; not that he ranks with them in a series, but they lay claim like him, only under a very different title, to a Divine parentage. Even if we had never sinned, and needed no redemption, there would be something in our very position as creatures which would draw us closer to him.

Having said that, St Paul has said enough for his immediate purposes. He has warned the angel-worshippers at Colossae that they are cheating the Divine Word of the honour due to him, as being the sole intermediary (if such a word can be used) in the work of Creation. But when he has reached that point, he digresses; it would not be St Paul if he did not digress. He goes on at once from the work of Creation to the work of Redemption, and insists that the Divine Word himself is the sole intermediary between God and Man, here too. Only, this time, as Incarnate; a close parallel is drawn between Christ as Creator and Christ as Redeemer, with a repetition of the actual words used. 'He too is that head whose body is the Church; it begins with him, since his was the first birth out of death; thus in every way the primacy was to become his. It was God's good pleasure to let all completeness dwell in him, and through him to win back all things, whether on earth or in heaven, into union with himself' (Col. i. 18 *sqq.*). The eternal Generation of the Divine Word is the first echo, as it were, which breaks the mysterious silence of heaven. And the Resurrection of Jesus Christ is the first echo which breaks the silence after the long sleep of death which has gone on undisturbed since Adam fell. Christ as God stood in a vague relation to all his creatures as in some sense their elder Brother; Christ as Man stands in a definite relation to them as the Head, the Clan-Chief in whom and with whom the whole Clan is mystically united; all creation is summed up in him. Nothing henceforward is complete without him; everything is re-born, as it was born, through him; everything lives, with a new life now, in him; he, the Centre of their being, is now also the Magnet which draws them back towards him. To him, whether as God or as Man, both priority and primacy belong.

We sometimes wonder why a single Person of the Blessed Trinity, and the Second Person rather than the First or the Third, should have brought us salvation. St Paul, to be sure, has no doubt that this, like every other divine act, is fundamentally the act of all three Persons at once; 'God was in Christ, reconciling the world to himself' (II Cor. v. 19), and by 'God' St Paul evidently means God the Father, except where the context makes such in interpretation unnatural. But for St Paul, as for St John, there was a clear appropriateness about the redemptive mission of the Divine Word; he who had made should remake us. And he will not begin to tell us the story of Christmas Day by taking us to our Lady's home at Nazareth, or to the stable at Bethlehem. Like St John, he will begin at the other end; or rather, he will begin at the Beginning. Its starting-point shall be a prologue in heaven.

And then, from that height, he swoops down suddenly to earth. He has assessed for us the meaning of the Incarnation in a passage we all know almost by heart, a famous passage in his epistle to the Philippians, 'His nature is, from the first, divine, and yet he did not see, in the rank of Godhead, a prize to be coveted; he dispossessed himself, and took the nature of a slave, fashioned in the likeness of men, and presenting himself to us in human form' (Phil. ii. 6) . There is metaphor, of course, in the terms St Paul uses; you cannot refer to such a subject without the use of metaphor. And I think you may say the picture St Paul has in his mind is that of a young prince who is determined to win the hearts of his subjects. Born in the purple, he is not dazzled by the pomp of royalty; he is prepared to lay all that aside. He cannot cease to be what he is, but he can voluntarily reduce himself to a condition in which the outward signs of royalty are foregone. And then the metaphor breaks down, as all metaphors must break down when you are referring to such a subject. The Divine Word really took upon himself the nature of Man, he, whose inalienable possession is the nature of God. If he came to us in human likeness, in human form, he was not practising a deception on our simplicity; he was Man.

So he came to us. We have seen what Man's position had been since Adam had fallen, how the fulfilment of the promises lingered, and the world seemed only to go from bad to worse; how the law was given, with no other result than to convict us more clearly of the guilt it could do nothing to remove. In that darkest hour the dawn came, as we are reminded in the thrilling epistle for the second Mass on Christmas Day: 'We, after all, were once like the rest of them, the dupes of error . . . our lives full of meanness and of envy, hateful, and hating one another. Then the kindness of God, our Saviour, dawned on us, his great love for man. He saved us, and it was not thanks to anything we had done for our own justification; in accordance with his own merciful design he saved us' (Tit. iii. 3 *sqq.*). All that happened in the interval had made no difference; we toiled away at our schoolroom tasks 'till the appointed time came. Then God sent out his Son on a mission to us. He took birth from a woman, took birth as a subject of the law, so as to ransom those who are subject to the law, and make us sons by adoption' (Gal. iv. 4). Born of a woman—yes, he was of our own flesh and blood, he had been through all the stages of human growth. Born under the law—yes, he had a historical context, belonged to a particular race, shared the culture of one particular country-side. St Paul knows how to come down to bedrock after all, to a particular cradle in a particular cave. But behind that, what a background of Providential design! He will not be satisfied until he has taken us back to the very origins.

ST PAUL AND CHRIST'S HUMANITY

No question of it, it is a great mystery we worship (I Tim. iii. 16).

WHEN WE talk about the life and death of our Lord Jesus Christ, we are using words in a special way. The word 'life-and-death' ought, if I may put it in that way, to be connected by hyphens; the two facts are intimately connected–indeed, you might almost say that you have a single fact there, viewed under two different aspects. Our Lord's death wasn't just the crown of his life; it was the bud of his life bursting into flower. Let me explain that phrase a little.

When somebody writes a book called 'The Life and Death of Lord Nelson', he is writing about two separate subjects. He is writing the life of a great admiral, who saved England. He is also writing about the death of a brave seaman who fell in battle. Oh, to be sure, Nelson's end was an appropriate one, from the spectacular, from the dramatic point of view. A poet could not have improved on the facts. But Nelson's life would have been that of a great admiral, even if he had lived as long as the Duke of Wellington. And Nelson's death would have been that of a brave seaman, if he had been a simple foremast hand. Whereas in our Lord's case we know that he came to earth to die. Most of us have seen that picture of Holman Hunt's, which represents our Lord in the carpenter's shop at Nazareth, when some chance arrangement of shadows has marked the wall behind him, where he stands with outstretched arms, in the figure of a cross. I don't know whether that picture is good art, but it is good theology. Our Lord's whole life is explained and is orientated by the death he foresees.

Because the two things are so closely connected, you will find a certain difference, I will not say of opinion but of emphasis, between Christian theologians. To some, his atoning death is the only reason, as far as we know, why he came into the world at all. The affront which our sins offered to God was infinite, and if full satisfaction was to be made for it, that could only be done by a Divine Victim; so the second Person of the Blessed Trinity became Man and suffered, in our stead, the penalty we had deserved. That explains the Incarnation; what more could you want? Others have laid more stress on Bethlehem, and less on Calvary; the mere fact of God taking Manhood upon him was enough of itself to heal and restore our fallen nature. They have considered it probable that there would have been an Incarnation, even if there had been no Fall.

Very roughly, you may say that the division is, as so often, a division between east and west; that it is the Latin Fathers who lay so much emphasis on the Atonement, the Greek Fathers who are more interested in the Incarnation. Very roughly, you may say that the party of the Atonement interprets the result of the Fall under a legal metaphor; the balance of the Divine Justice has been disturbed, and there must be compensation before it is adjusted. Whereas the party of the Incarnation interprets the result of the Fall in organic terms; human nature has been fatally wounded, and it can only be restored by being grafted somehow into the Divine Nature; it is something like a transfusion of blood. Very roughly, you may say that one party takes its cue from our Lord's own account of his mission, 'the Son of Man came to give his life as a ransom for the lives of many' (Matt. xx. 28); the other takes its cue from that other account which our Lord gave, 'I have come so that they may have life, and have it more abundantly' (John x. 10).

So the stream of Christian tradition is divided, though only, as I say, as a matter of emphasis. On which side does St Paul come down? Which party claims his support?

It would be impossible to deny that St Paul describes the work of our salvation, sometimes, under legal metaphors. You cannot, after all, speak of redemption, as St Paul often does, without using a legal metaphor. In the Old Testament Almighty God is often described as redeeming his people, in a sense which generally passes over our heads. The Jewish law was very careful about hereditary titles to landed property, and if a piece of ground was up for sale, there was always somebody who had the first claim to be the purchaser, because he was the head of the family to which it originally belonged.

Only if he could not or would not buy it might it be sold to a stranger; you get that prominently mentioned in the Book of Ruth. In the mind of the Hebrew prophets, ever since their deliverance from Egypt, Israel belonged specially to God, by a kind of hereditary right; and when Israel was conquered by its enemies, when its people went into exile, it meant that God's ancient inheritance was (so to speak) up for sale. Surely then he, as having the first claim upon it, would buy in this precious possession of his, instead of letting it go to strangers! That sense of the word passes over into the New Testament, and when Zachary blesses the God of Israel for having visited his people and wrought their redemption, that sense will have been uppermost in his mind. And quite possibly St Paul, too, has it in mind when he writes to the Galatians about God sending his Son into the world to buy up those who were subject to the law (Gal. iv. 5); salvation was offered first to the Jews, because God had proprietary rights over them as his own people.

But it is not merely in this vague sense of proprietorship that Jesus Christ is said to redeem us. 'A great price was paid to ransom you,' St Paul writes to the Corinthians, and again, 'A price was paid to redeem you' (I Cor. vi. 20; vii. 23); here, perhaps, he is thinking of slaves being set at liberty, and drawing special attention to the fact that this can only be done by the payment of a ransom. What ransom it was that was paid to deliver us from the bondage of sin is a matter that admits of no doubt; the price paid for our liberty was a human life.

The idea of a life being given up by way of ransom was, of course, familiar to Jewish thought; it entered into the whole philosophy of sacrifice. Our Lord himself, as the first-born Son of his Mother, had to be redeemed by the slaughter of a turtle-dove, or two young pigeons. And he himself, as we saw just now, told us that the Son of Man came to give his life as a ransom for the lives of many—instead of many, if you insist on the full flavour of the word. St Paul does not imitate that turn of speech; he doesn't say that our Lord gave up his life in our stead, only that he gave it up on our behalf—perhaps a significant variation of language. We have reminded ourselves that, in St Paul's language, Christ Incarnate is the elder Brother of humanity; what a temptation for him to point to the position of the first-born in Jewish law! In theory, the first-born of every man or beast was forfeit as a sacrifice to Almighty God. In theory, then, you may say that the eldest son of a family gave up his life as a ransom for the lives of the rest; how apt a parallel that would have been! But nowhere does St Paul's language suggest it; he avoids, for the most part, the idea of a substituted Victim. Although he once refers to our Lord as a paschal Victim (I Cor. v. 7), offered on our behalf, he never uses the word 'lamb'; it is St John and St Peter who tell us about the Lamb of God. Why that is, perhaps we shall see later.

At the same time, you cannot deny that the Death of our Lord Jesus Christ is central to St Paul's theology. He is always for drawing attention to the Cross; he will make his boast of nothing else, however much the Jews shrink, however much the Gentiles mock, at the sight of its ignominy. Indeed, I think you can say that to St Paul the Cross suggested, not so much the idea of suffering, as the idea of publicity. He tells the Galatians that Christ has been advertised to them, hanging on a cross (Gal. iii. 1); and later in the same epistle he says that through it the world has been crucified to him, and he to the world (Gal. vi. 14); it was a kind of legal instrument, setting it on record that the world has nothing to do with Paul, that Paul has nothing to do with the world, in future. Yes, a legal instrument; St Paul is never afraid of talking lawyer's language. And above all the Cross is a document which sets on record the establishment of peace between God and man, like those old cairns and pillars which the patriarchs used to raise when they wanted to make a covenant. God's forgiveness means that he cancelled the deed which excluded us, the decree made to our prejudice, swept it out of the way, by nailing it to his cross (Col. ii. 14)—the cross, you see, is still the notice-board of the new covenant. A covenant of peace; it was through the cross that he abolished all feuds, including the old feud between Jew and Gentile; 'both sides, united in a single body, he would reconcile to God through his cross' (Eph. ii. 16). It was a legal instrument; you must not preach the gospel with devices of human rhetoric, for that would be cancelling—it is the plain meaning of the word—cancelling the cross of Christ (I Cor. i. 17).

That notion perhaps throws light on a very curious

phrase used in the epistle to the Colossians, about 'making peace through the blood of his cross' (Col. i. 20). It is all very well to say that it simply means 'his blood shed on the cross'; but if St Paul simply meant that, it would have been easy to say that. Surely he means us to have before our eyes the picture of a cross stained with blood; surely he means us to connect it with the picture you get in the epistle to the Hebrews, of Moses sprinkling the book with blood when he founded the old Covenant (Heb. ix. 19). Either testament was sealed with blood; the old, when Moses sprinkled the document which enshrined it, the new, when those red drops trickled down the upright wooden beam. The new covenant has the cross for its parchment, blood for its ink.

I don't mean to suggest that St Paul's thought was in any way out of harmony with our traditional Catholic doctrine of the Atonement; that he didn't look upon our Lord's death as the payment of a ransom; didn't see a foreshadowing of it in the Old Testament sacrifices. No, when Easter came round he would write to the Corinthians about Christ our paschal Victim (I Cor. v. 7), and in his farewell speech to the elders of Ephesus he would refer to the Church as that flock which God won for himself at the price of his own blood (Acts xx. 28). But that way of talking wasn't habitual with him; possibly because the old sacrifices always suggested to him the idea of substitution. Even when you offered sacrifice for a fault committed, and laid your hands on the head of the victim by way of transferring your guilt from yourself to it, that was only a kind of legal ceremony; the fact remained that you had committed a fault, and it was the goat, not you, that suffered for it. Now, we understand very little about the mystery of our redemption, and it isn't unnatural that we should represent it to ourselves as a transaction of that kind. God consented to treat our Lord's death as an expiation for our fault, although the suffering, and the acceptance of suffering, were not ours but his. The reason, I think, why St Paul didn't use that language was because it didn't match his outlook on the Incarnation. The Incarnation effected a mystical union between Christ and his Church which made it misleading to talk as if our Lord were one thing and his Church another. He didn't suffer instead of a guilty race; he identified himself, not by a legal fiction, but by a real (though mystical) union, with a guilty race, and suffered as its representative.

All through the epistle to the Galatians, especially, this idea seems to be pressing on the mind of the apostle, the identification of Christ with the Christian. He, Paul, has no longer any life of his own, it is Christ that lives in him; with Christ he hangs on the cross (Gal. ii. 20), so that the world is crucified to him, and he to the world (Gal. vi. 14); he bears on his body the scars of the Crucified (Gal. vi. 17). And this intimate indwelling is not for a privileged few, it is general to the Christian community; the apostle feels something like the pains of childbirth while he waits for Christ to be fully formed in his spiritual children (Gal. iv. 17). It is only a matter of development; already, it seems, they are Christ in embryo. 'All you who have been baptized in Christ's name have put on the person of Christ; no more Jew or Gentile, no more slave and freeman, no more male and female; you are all one person in Jesus Christ' (Gal. iii. 28).

Bethlehem means Christ born in Man, and Man reborn in Christ. Calvary means that Mankind has died in the person of Christ, it means also that Christ has died in the name of mankind; not instead of us, as our substitute, but in our name, as our representative. He identified himself with us; I do not know where you can get clearer evidence of St Paul's view in this matter than a passage in his second letter to the Corinthians, where he argues thus: 'If one man died on behalf of all, then all thereby became dead men' (II Cor. v. 14). If he had written 'instead of all', the argument would be nonsense; if one man dies instead of another, like Sidney Carton in the *Tale of Two Cities,* then we infer that the other man remains alive. But St Paul does not think of Christ as dying *for* us in that sense; rather as dying in the capacity of our representative, so that when he died we died with him. For St Paul, Christ did not die in order that we might live; he died in order that we might die. In what sense, we shall see in a moment.

It was not, then, by a kind of legal fiction that the sufferings of Jesus Christ, his, not ours, were allowed to count as reparation for our sins, ours, not his. It was in virtue of a mystical union with mankind that he was qualified to act as mankind's representative. And in this mystical sense you can even say that our guilt was transferred to him. At least, it is difficult to read any other meaning into that curious verse of the Galatian epistle, where St Paul writes: 'Those who take their stand on the law are all under a curse. . . . From this curse invoked by the law Christ has ransomed us, by himself becoming, for our sakes, an accursed thing' (Gal. iii. 10, 14). There is a rather far-fetched allusion, here, to a text in Deuteronomy: we need not go into the details of all that; the fact remains that St Paul is prepared to describe our Lord as becoming 'an accursed thing'. And in writing to the Corinthians he uses an even more startling phrase: 'Christ never knew sin, and God made him into sin for us, so that in him we might be turned into the holiness of God' (II Cor. v. 21). Christ never knew sin—oh, it is all right, St Paul is not being heretical. It was impossible that our Lord should feel, personally, the consciousness of guilt. Yet our Lord had so identified himself with us, that what hung on the Cross was, to the mystic's view, a load of guilt. To be sure, the Hebrew language made it easier for St Paul to talk like that; in Hebrew, the word for 'sin' can also be used to mean 'a victim for sin'. But the underlying sense of what St Paul says is plain enough; our Lord for our sakes became sin, so that through him we might become innocence. It is not enough to think of the Cross, like the hymn *Vexilla regis,* as a pair of scales with our sin on one side and our Lord's Sacrifice on the other. We are to think of the Cross as a pillory, upon which he who summed up the whole of humanity summed up the whole guilt of humanity, hung there as a kind of impersonation of guilt, and by the destruction of his body destroyed the body of our sin.

We think of our Lord's death as the meritorious cause of our deliverance from guilt; we say 'Christ died in order that we might arise again from the death of sin.' St Paul, usually though not always, thinks of Christ's death as the exemplary cause of our deliverance from guilt; he says 'Christ died, and with him and in him we died to our sins; Christ rose again, and with him and in him we rose again to a new life of innocence'. When he says 'We died to our sins', he is using language with which we are unfamiliar, but after all, as he points out, it is the language of common life. Death cancels all obligations; and we, who were debtors under the law, and bankrupt debtors, because we were bound to keep the law and we couldn't, escaped from our obligations by dying with Christ. We are dead, and our life is hidden with Christ in God; our creditor, the law of Moses, cannot get at us now.

Well, we haven't yet answered the question we set out to answer: Which school of Christian thinkers did St Paul belong to? Did he see the Incarnation as something important in itself, or as something important because of what it led up to—the Atonement? If you had put the question in that way, I don't think he would have known what to answer; because to him the Atonement was part of the Incarnation, one aspect of it, one mood of it, not to be isolated in contrast with the rest. 'All I know,' he would have told you, 'is that when Jesus Christ became Man, you and I were somehow mystically identified with him. His life, not just by the circumstances of it but by the whole purpose and dedication of it, led up to his death on the cross. And when he died, you and I, mystically identified with him, became dead to our old life of sin and disobedience; we were buried with him, and rose again with him into a new life, in which God is our sun and Christ is the air we breathe. Was it the Incarnation, or the Atonement, that did that? I cannot tell; all I know is that my life is the faith I have in the Son of God, who loved me, and gave himself for me' (Gal. ii. 20).

ST PAUL ON THE MYSTICAL BODY

May he be glorified in the Church, and in Christ Jesus (Eph. iii. 21).

THE WORDS I quoted to you at the end of my last sermon were a favourite text with the old-fashioned Evangelicals, 'the Son of God, who loved me and gave himself for me'. The reason is not far to seek; for the Evangelical, everything depends on an inner conviction that Jesus Christ has died for him personally, and this text was the ideal expression of it. What they omitted to tell us is that it stands alone in St Paul's writings; everywhere else, I think, he insists that Christ died for us, gave himself for us.

The point I am making is that St Paul is, if ever a man was, a churchman. St Peter, curiously, doesn't use the word 'church' in his epistles at all; St Paul uses it more than sixty times—in fact, if you are reading him in the Vulgate, you will find that the word occurs almost on every page. But it is not merely that he often has occasion to mention the Church; more than once he seems to mention it where you would have thought there was no occasion to do so at all. In those words, for example, which I gave you just now as my text, why was it necessary for him, if he wanted to end up the chapter with a doxology, to phrase it in this extraordinary way? 'May he be glorified in the Church, and in Christ Jesus'—as if the Church took rank with her Incarnate Master as one of the organs of God's praise; nay, took first rank, with her Incarnate Master second? It bothered the copyists, and some of them left out the word 'and'. If you look in the Authorized Version you will find, 'to him be glory *in* the Church *by* Christ Jesus'—it has even altered the preposition. But there is no doubt that ours was the true reading, 'in the Church and in Christ Jesus'. St Paul's mind is so occupied with the thought of the Church, God's splendid tapestry of Jew and Gentile, that he can think of nothing else for the moment, and for once the Person of Jesus Christ comes in as a kind of afterthought.

Our Lord doesn't seem to have talked much about his Church; his favourite way of describing the Christian commonwealth was 'the kingdom of God' or 'the kingdom of heaven'. But on two occasions, at least, he did talk about the 'Church', and the memory it will have called up in the minds of his disciples was the assembly, the 'gathering together' of his ancient people the Jews, when he brought them out of Egypt into Chanaan. In old days, God had chosen a particular nation to be his Assembly; now he, Jesus Christ, would have an assembly of his own, no longer merely national in its membership. When the apostles took to preaching the Gospel in Greek, they didn't call this new Assembly a 'gathering together', because that word 'synagogue', had already been appropriated by the Jews. They called it the ecclesia, the 'outcalling' of Christ. This was evidently, from the first, the technical way of describing the Christian body, and for the most part the New Testament authors use it in a severely technical sense. They don't seem to get excited about it; it is merely a convenient way of describing, either the total number of Christians in some particular area, or the total number of Christians in the world. Three times out of four, the word 'congregation' would answer just as well. Strange, that our Lord's defiant utterance, 'on this rock I will build my church', finds no echo, for example, in the Acts of the Apostles! No, I am wrong, there is one. 'Keep watch, then, over God's church, in which the Holy Spirit has made you bishops; you are to be the shepherds of that flock which he won for himself at the price of his own blood' (Acts xx. 28). But it comes in a speech reported verbatim, and the speaker is St Paul.

For St Paul, especially when he is writing to the Ephesians and to the Colossians, the Church is a mysterious entity with a life of its own, something much more than the sum of its members. He calls it, for example, the 'pillar and foundation upon which the truth rests' (Tim. iii. 15); already, in that dawn of believing, heresy begins to threaten, and the appeal from it is made, not precisely to the apostles who still lived, but to the *Ecclesia Docens,* human in her membership, and yet wiser than ourselves. But that is a solitary reference, late in his career. For the most part, he is lyrical about the Church not as the touchstone of truth, but as the focus of unity. We Christians are one in Christ, and the Church is both ideally the expression of that unity, and in practice the arena for realizing it.

Oh, I know, St Paul will talk to you about 'the churches' of Asia or 'the churches' of Macedonia, in a way that is apt to make you think of them as so many independent units, vaguely federated. But even as he does that, if you will look more closely at the context, St Paul is deliberately overriding these local boundaries. He is appealing to the various 'churches' to subscribe to a charity of his; a fund he is raising to help the impoverished 'church' at Jerusalem. And if you will read the eighth and ninth chapters of his second epistle to the Corinthians, you will see what importance he attached to it, and why. 'The administration of this public service', he says, 'does more than supply the needs of the saints; it yields, besides, a rich harvest of thanksgiving in the name of the Lord. . . . They will intercede, too, on your behalf, as the abundant measure of grace which God bestows on you warms their hearts towards you' (II Cor. ix. 12, 14). This very practical form of intercourse was the best way, he saw, of knitting together the hearts of Christian people who live remote from one another; he calls it 'the communion' (II Cor. viii. 4; ix. 13), calls it by that sacred name by which, already, men referred to participation in the Holy Eucharist. That was what St Paul thought of second collections.

For him, there was one Church, and its unity was diffused everywhere, like the air we breathe. He is not content to talk about 'the church' in this or that town; he will talk about 'the church' in so-and-so's household (e.g., Rom. xvi. 5)—the little group of Christian slaves, perhaps not always with a Christian master, who met to say their prayers together were a cross-section of Christendom, a little microcosm in which the Church was represented, as the sun may be reflected in a puddle. The Church itself was a glorious reconciliation of human differences; in it there was neither Jew nor Gentile, neither slave nor freeman, neither barbarian nor Scythian, neither male nor female, all were one person in Christ (Gal. iii. 28). And each family, in the same way, had its differences to be reconciled; 'I call upon thee, Euodia, and I call upon thee, Syntyche, to make common cause in the Lord' (Phil. iv. 2). Who were they? We don't know; we don't even know whether Euodia was male or female—perhaps St Paul didn't; but their bickerings were not to go on. And in the same way, he will put an end to rivalries in this or that congregation; everybody is to do his own job, and not be envious of the next man. How small-minded they were, even those first Christians! But St Paul is not discouraged by it; here is an excellent opportunity, he thinks, for realizing on a small scale the glorious comprehensiveness of Christ's Church.

How does he think of that Church, seen in its full extension? Three metaphors he has for it, all familiar enough, but all worth looking into. For him, it is the bride of Christ; it is the building of which Christ is corner-stone; it is the body of which Christ is head.

It is not a matter for surprise that St Paul should have pictured the relations between Christ and his Church under the image of man and wife. The Church was the people of Christ, exactly as the Synagogue was the people of God; and it is a commonplace, when you are reading the Old Testament prophets, to find Israel referred to as the bride of his youth, false to him now. 'And thou with many lovers hast played the wanton,' so runs the appeal of Jeremias, 'yet come back to me, the Lord says, and thou shalt find welcome' (Jer. iii. 1) . No wonder that St Paul should employ the same kind of metaphor; 'My jealousy on your behalf is the jealousy of God himself; I have betrothed you to Christ, so that no other but he should claim you, his bride without spot; and now I am anxious about you' (II Cor. xi. 2) . And so, in writing to the Ephesians, he represents our Lord himself as shewing his love for the Church by giving up his life for it, so that he might summon it into his presence, the Church in all its beauty; it was to be holy, it was to be spotless. All that we should expect; it is what follows, in this Ephesian passage, that makes us rub our eyes.

It is very characteristic of St Paul that he is not setting out to read the Ephesians a lesson in his doctrine of the Church. No, the Church comes in merely by way of illustration; what he is setting out to do is to make the husbands at Ephesus treat their wives less selfishly! But he is not content to say, 'Christ treated his bride the Church so lovingly, you men ought to treat your wives lovingly, in imitation of him'. He says, apparently, that a man ought to be a good husband merely from self-interest; after all, the wife is part of her husband just as the Church is part of Christ. 'That is how a man ought to love his wife, as if she were his own body; in loving his wife, a man is but loving himself. And so it is with Christ and his Church; we are limbs of his body, flesh and bone, we belong to him. That is why a man will leave his father and mother and will cling to his wife, and the two will become one flesh. Yes, those words are a high mystery, and I am applying them here to Christ and his Church' (Eph. v. 28, 29, 33).

Useless, perhaps, to ask St Paul which is the premiss from which he starts, which is the conclusion he reaches. Is he telling us that man and wife are one thing, therefore Christ and his Church are one thing? Or is he telling us that Christ and his Church are one thing, therefore man and wife ought to be one thing? I doubt if you can hold St Paul down to a syllogism like that. Rather, he sees the two truths simultaneously, either mirrored in the other. Either truth is mystical, although in the case of the husband there is a moral application; the grace of the sacrament, here as elsewhere, has to be lived up to. What concerns us, is that our mystical union with Christ is essentially a corporate one; St Paul has betrothed the Corinthians to Christ not as so many brides (the language of a later mysticism) but as a single bride; it is in and through our identification with the Church that we are identified with Christ.

The point is still more clearly emphasized by an alternative image which the Apostle gives us in this same letter to the Ephesians, that of a spiritual building. 'Apostles and prophets are the foundation on which you were built, and the chief corner-stone of it is Jesus Christ himself. In him the whole fabric is bound together, as it grows into a temple, dedicated to the Lord; in him you too are being built in with the rest, so that God may find in you a dwelling-place for his Spirit' (Eph. ii. 20–22). Two minor difficulties occur to the reader, neither of which has great importance for our present purposes. Are the prophets in question the prophets of the Old Testament? More probably those of the New; not in the sense that they were ever recognized as taking rank, merely as prophets, in the hierarchy of the Church, but in their capacity as preachers; 'he who prophesies', we are told elsewhere, 'builds up the church' (I Cor. xiv. 4). Again, does 'the foundation of the apostles' mean a foundation consisting of the apostles, or a foundation which the apostles lay, as in the third chapter of the first Corinthian letter (I Cor. iii. 10)? I doubt very much if St Paul stopped to ask himself which of the two he meant.

The metaphor is a common one; St Peter uses it (I Pet. ii. 4), perhaps with some memory of Caesarea Philippi. St Paul, in writing to the Ephesians, has a particular application for it; he has been talking, all through the chapter, about the vocation of the Gentiles, and he represents Christ as the corner-stone, *lapis angularis qui facis utraque unum;* in him Jew and Gentile, hitherto distinct, meet and are bound into one. The key-word of the passage is a word which only occurs in one other place in Greek literature; 'the whole fabric is bound together'—perhaps we ought to say 'is dove-tailed together', if we want a vivid translation. The apparently ill-assorted people fitting in together after all—that was how St. Paul saw the ideal Christian congregation, each man following his own aptitudes and doing his own job without, somehow, feeling inclined to criticize the way the other man was doing his. And so it is here, on a larger scale; Jew and Gentile, why shouldn't they mix, in Christ? Why shouldn't different nations, different cultures, each have their own contribution to make, for the perfecting of Christ's building? All that, perhaps, St Paul would have developed; even, perhaps, developed the other side of it, as it is developed in the hymn *Caelestis urbs;* the shaping, the fashioning of each stone, *fabri polita malleo,* which has to be done before it fits into its right niche, the retrenchment of personality which we call mortification. . . . But he doesn't develop all that; and if he doesn't, I think it is because he didn't like taking his metaphor from stones and mortar; they were dead things merely superimposed on one another, and St Paul liked to think of Christian people as living things, growing out of one another.

Living things, growing out of one another—so, in his epistle to the Romans, he compares the fusion of Jew and Gentile in the Church not to a feat of architecture, but to a feat of gardening. They are not two walls, meeting at a common angle, they are two growths of olive, one wild, one fruit-bearing, and the wild growth of the Gentiles is grafted into the fruitful Jewish stock (Rom. xi. 17 *sqq.*). That was well enough, but he would go deeper yet. I said just now that the word which I translated 'dove-tailed' only occurs twice in Greek literature. It does; once in Ephesians ii. 21, and once in Ephesians iv. 16. In this latter passage he takes the same word and deliberately grafts it on to an organic metaphor. It is as if he were saying 'Dove-tailed, yes; I told you just now that we were dove-tailed into one another like different parts of a building. But really it is a closer union than that; we are dove-tailed into one another like different parts of the human body'. So it is that you get the magnificent passage in which he tells us that we are to grow up, through charity, into a due proportion with Christ, who is our head. How good his metaphors are! Because of course a child's head is out of proportion, it is waiting for the rest of the body to grow up and match it; so Christ and we. 'On him all the body depends; it is organized and unified by each contact with the source which supplies it; and thus, each limb receiving the active power it needs, it achieves its natural growth, building itself up (he is betrayed into the old, discarded image again)—building itself up through charity.'

He is not really happy, you see, about his doctrine of the Church until he has expressed it in terms of the Mystical Body. As our Lord had a natural body, which must be swaddled and suckled by our Lady at Bethlehem, so he has a mystical body which must take shape and receive nourishment and so grow up into the perfect thing he wants it to be. This image is the same, yet not the same, as our Lord's own image of the True Vine (John xv. 1–6). The same, because there too you get the sense of an intimate connexion; the branch does not depend upon its parent stock more wholly than we depend on our incorporation into Christ; does not perish more surely if it is lopped off than we do if, most miserably, we allow ourselves to be separated from him. And yet not the same, for our Lord is thinking only of our relations with him, not of our relations with one another. Each of the people to whom he is speaking—and they, remember, were the great princes of his Church—is only a twig, you can hardly call it a branch, of the one Vine; the Vine, all of it except the twigs, is himself. All that tells you the truth about our union with Christ; it does not tell you the full truth about our union in Christ. For St Paul, Christ is the head, and we are members of the body, depending not only upon him but upon one another, as the members of a human body do. 'The body, after all, consists not of one organ but of many; if the foot should say, I am not the hand, and therefore I do not belong to the body, does it belong to the body any the less for that? There was to be no want of unity in the body; all the different parts of it were to make each other's welfare their common care. If one part is suffering, all the rest suffer with it; if one part is treated with honour, all the rest find pleasure in it. And you are

ST PAUL ON THE RISEN LIFE OF THE CHRISTIAN

You, by baptism, have been united with his burial; united, too, with his resurrection, through your faith in that exercise of power by which God raised him from the dead (Col. ii. 12).

WE HAVE SEEN how St Paul loves to dwell on the union, the self-identification, of Christ with his Church. The Church is his body, 'the completion of him who everywhere and in all things is complete' (Eph. i. 23) —nothing less than that paradox will content St Paul. The Humanity of our Blessed Lord is the most absolute achievement in God's creation; you cannot think of it but as a thing utterly complete in itself. And yet, if you look at the whole question from another angle, the Sacred Humanity would be incomplete without us; it was for our sakes he came down from heaven, and if, *per impossibile,* nobody from our Blessed Lady downwards had believed in him or accepted the gift of salvation from him, the purpose of the Incarnation would have remained unrealized. St Paul is very fond of this word 'completion', and it may be true that he was using, in an orthodox sense, the language of those heretics whose false teaching was a danger to the Church at Colossae. But I sometimes wonder whether it may not have suggested to him, besides, a familiar image. St Paul came from Tarsus, a place of ships and seamen; less than a century before, it had been the great center of piracy in the Mediterranean. And the Greeks talked about 'completing' a ship where we should talk of 'manning' a ship; described the crew of a ship as its 'completion'. Did he, perhaps, at the back of his mind, think of the Sacred Humanity as a ship, an Ark, which would have meant nothing if there had been no crew to sail it?

On the other side, hard as it may be to think of ourselves as the completing of Christ's nature, there is no difficulty whatever in realizing that he is the completion of ours. 'In Christ,' says the Apostle, 'the whole plenitude of Deity is embodied, and in him you find your completion. . . . You, by baptism, have been united to his burial, united, too, with his resurrection' (Col. ii. 10, 12). Man's nature, ever since the Fall, incapable of achieving his clear destiny, conscious, however dimly, of the desire to please God, yet with no apparatus for doing it—how could anything be so manifestly incomplete? Compare him, if you will, to a ship bound for some distant port, with no complement of sailors to man her. . . . You would almost expect to find St Paul comparing Christian baptism with the rescue of Noe and his sons in the ark. But he doesn't; it is St Peter who does that (I Pet. iii. 20). For St Paul, the type of baptism is the people of Israel, led out from its Egyptian bondage through the Red Sea.

That analogy will have been in the minds of Christian

people from the first; it could hardly be otherwise. Our Lord suffered death at the time of the great Jewish feast; evidently he meant us to understand that he was being sacrificed for us as our Paschal Victim, meant us to understand that the escape of Israel from Egypt by way of the Red Sea was a type of Christian baptism, cutting us off, as if by a wall of water, from our dead past. The hymn *Exultet,* which we sing on Holy Saturday, a hymn that in its whole inspiration takes you right back to the very beginnings of Christendom, is full of that imagery. 'This night, long ago, thou didst rescue the sons of Israel, our fathers, out of Egypt, over the Red Sea bidding them pass dry-shod; none but this, with pillar of cloud to enlighten it, shadow of man's sin could purge away.' So we bless the candle that is the type of our Lord himself, that will be dipped into the new Font, and make it pregnant with the power of spiritual re-birth. All that, or at least the doctrinal kernel of all that, St Paul knew about; we learn as much from a casual reference, a single word of one of his letters—how prodigal he is of unexploited allusion, throwing out a significant word to us, and passing on!

He is warning the Corinthians that it is a fatal error to presume on one's grace; you must co-operate with it energetically; he who thinks he stands firmly should beware of a fall. And he illustrates that by recalling the infidelities of the Jewish people in the wilderness; they (he says) could sin and did sin in spite of the great graces bestowed on them. Had they not been saved from the pursuit of their enemies by the cloud that overhung their camp, by the waters of the Red Sea which closed behind them? Only he does not use that phrase, 'Saved from the pursuit of their enemies'; his words are, 'All alike, in the cloud and in the sea, were baptized into Moses' fellowship' (I Cor. x. 2). What he means, evidently, is that Christian baptism, intimately connected with our Lord's Resurrection and with the feast of our Lord's Resurrection, is the fulfilment of a type; it puts a distance between us and our sins, isolates us in the close unity of Christian fellowship; we too are like men who have escaped from bondage, rallied now under a divine leadership. On all that background of his thought the Apostle just lifts, as it were, the corner of a curtain when, almost absent-mindedly, he calls the crossing of the Red Sea a baptism.

But of course, from his point of view, the type is only a feeble image, it doesn't do justice to the situation. The Israelites, when they escaped from Egypt, escaped with their lives; it is not so with Christian baptism. To be baptized is to undergo a mystical death, in union with our Lord's death on the cross, a mystical burial in union with his burial, a mystical resurrection in union with his resurrection. We have been taken up into Christ's death, in our baptism, we have been buried with him, died like him, that so, just as Christ was raised up by his Father's power from the dead, we too might live and move in a new kind of existence'. We are grafted into a new stock; 'our former nature has been crucified with him, and the living power of our guilt destroyed, so that we are the slaves of sin no longer. Guilt makes no more claim on a man who is dead' (Rom. vi. 4). Do not ask St Paul whether this mystical death sets us free from the old law, or sets us free from guilt; it is the same process–the burden we carried when we were still unregenerate was that of an obligation we could not meet; the law and our sinfulness played into one another's hands, were the upper and nether millstone which ground us between them. Now it is all right; we are dead, and death cancels all obligations. Elsewhere, pressing his imagery still more boldly, he tells us that we are dead, and our life is hidden away with Christ in God (Col. iii. 3); we take refuge from our pursuers, and our hiding-place is a tomb.

Not that St Paul is unacquainted with that other and more familiar imagery which describes baptism as washing us clean from our sins; 'he saved us with the cleansing power which gives us new birth' (Tit. iii. 5). But that is not his favourite way of talking; and, I think, for two reasons. Washing is something external to ourselves, we get rid of something on the surface that was never really part of us: whereas the grace of baptism goes down to the very roots of our nature, restores us to a new kind of existence. And washing is a process we may repeat as often as we will; baptism is not like that, it is a single, crucial moment, like the moment of death. Dead, buried, and risen with Christ, that is our state, when we have been baptized. We must not imagine, when St Paul uses a legal metaphor about death cancelling all strongly on the catastrophic effects of the new birth, he is pleading with us to live up to it and be worthy of it. 'You must be quit, now, of the old self whose way of life you remember, the self that wasted its aim on false dreams. . . . You must be quit of the old self, and the habits that went with it; you must be clothed in the new self, that is being refitted all the time for closer knowledge, so that the image of the God who created it is its pattern' (Eph. iv. 22; Col. iii. 9). He tells us that we have got to get rid of the old self, not that we are rid of it. The doctrine of the new birth is not an All-clear signal to tell us that the struggle with sin is all over. It is a call to arms, bidding us enter on the struggle, because at last we have a chance of victory. 'You must not make your bodily powers over to sin. . . . Sin will not be able to play the master over you any longer; you serve grace now, not the law' (Rom. vi. 13, 14).

You serve grace now, not the law—that means, evidently and most importantly, a better chance in the struggle; the law does but set before us a high standard, which we despair of achieving, grace enables us. But something else, I think, is implied. When you serve the law, you serve it, inevitably, in a legal spirit, unwillingly, grudgingly, according to the letter. When you serve free grace, you serve it in a spirit of freedom; you enter (as we say) into the spirit of it, cooperate, gladly and generously, with its designs for you. That contrast between doing God's will because you have got to and doing God's will because you want to is more explicitly set forth elsewhere. When the Jews were rescued from their bondage in Egypt, they emerged (you might almost say) from one bondage into another; they were God's slaves now instead of Pharao's, obeying him, if they obeyed him at all, blindly, unquestioningly, as they obeyed Pharao. But when the grace of Jesus Christ came to us, it was no longer, this time, a mere change of masters. 'The spirit you have now received is not, as of old, a spirit of slavery, to govern you by fear; it is the spirit of adoption, which makes us cry out Abba, Father!' (Rom. viii. 15). It is the same principle which our Lord himself had taught, though with a slightly different emphasis, when he told his apostles, 'I do not speak of you now as my servants; a servant is one who does not understand what his master is about, whereas I have made known to you all that my Father has told me, and so I have called you my friends' (John xv. 15). If the practice of the Christian religion seems to you and me something uncommonly like drudgery, that is our fault; it was not meant to be. The only really Christian attitude is to obey God with the dutifulness of loving sons, is to follow Christ with the loyalty of devoted friends.

With baptism, we escape from the sense of mere law-abidingness which afflicted us under the Old Covenant, a dull, negative thing, and become conscious of an active principle working in us instead. What is this active principle? Nothing other than the Holy Spirit; where the Lord's Spirit is, there is liberty (II Cor. iii. 17). We have not, after all, finished the story when we have reminded ourselves that Christ died and was buried, and rose again from the dead. The natural corollary of our Lord's rising from the dead is his Ascension. He went down to the lower regions of earth; and he who so went down is no other than he who has gone up, high above all the heavens, to fill creation wth his presence. He has given gifts to men—so one of the psalms had prophesied, in the version of it which St Paul knew; Pentecost, in its turn, is the corollary of the Ascension (Eph. iv. 8–10). And now he, who fills all things with his presence, has poured out the love of God in our hearts by the Holy Spirit, whom we have received. Confirmation, in those days when so many catechumens were grown men, followed close on baptism, just as Pentecost followed close on the Resurrection. 'We too, all of us, have been baptized into a single body by the power of a single Spirit, . . . we have all been given to drink at a single source, the one Spirit'—you have two processes there, but they are complementary; how should a body exist without breath in it? We are to live by the spirit as naturally (I had almost said, as unconsciously) as our physical bodies live by the breath we breathe.

To live by the Spirit, as, in ideal at least, Christians should, is sometimes referred to as 'walking about in the Spirit' (Gal. v. 16); strolling about at our pleasure (that is the notion of the Hebrew metaphor), taking our ease, 'finding ourselves' in that element. Sometimes it is referred to as being 'led about' by the Spirit, as if the responsibility for every decision was taken out of our hands, so instinctively do we respond to the least touch of the divine guidance (Rom. viii. 14). That is why, as we were reminding ourselves just now, the new covenant of grace is a covenant of freedom. The life of the spirit, St Paul tells us, has appetites of its own, diametrically opposed to the appetites of unregenerate nature and therefore, ideally, excluding them (Gal. v. 18 *sqq.*). A combat the Christian life may be at any level; if we find it a conflict, that is because it is being lived at a low level—the reign of the Spirit in us is incomplete.

I say, ideally; it is quite evident that even in St Paul's day there could be, and there was, maladjustment in Christian lives. All through his letters to the Corinthians, that is his chief anxiety; the exceptional gifts of the Holy Spirit—less exceptional then than now—such as prophecy, healing of sickness, speaking with unknown tongues, abounded at Corinth; but where were those other qualities, gifts of the Holy Spirit no less, that made for the building up of the Church, the spirit of discipline, the spirit of humility, above all, the spirit of charity (I Cor. xii. 31)? This doubt on the apostle's part will account for the way in which he always includes in his list of spiritual gifts various aptitudes which have nothing of the abnormal, nothing of the sensational about them; there is a charisma of preaching the word, a charisma of teaching, a charisma, even, of financial administration (I Cor. xii. 28; Eph. iv. 11). Any quality, he insists, which makes us useful members of the Church is bestowed upon us by that same Spirit who enables us to prophesy, to speak with tongues. The craving for powers which are unusual, which are apparently supernatural, is for St Paul a kind of vulgarity.

It is perhaps possible to trace the same warning when he tells us that 'the Spirit comes to the aid of our weakness; when we do not know what prayer to offer, to pray as we ought, the Spirit himself intercedes for us, with groans beyond all utterance' (Rom. viii. 26). He does not mean that the groans are indescribable, but that they find no outlet in words. More impressive, to him, than all the outcry of prophet and glossolalist was that inner, silent experience of the mystic who feels that the business of prayer is being taken out of his own hands, that the Holy Spirit is praying in him.

'Abba, Father'—why does St Paul say that? Why does he give you the title first in Aramaic and then in Greek? He does it twice over; the Galatians, too, are reminded that God has sent out the Spirit of his Son into our hearts, crying out in us, Abba, Father (Rom. viii. 15; Gal. iv. 6). Is he consciously quoting from St Mark's account of Gethsemani, where alone (perhaps by way of an editorial note) the Aramaic word is given and then translated? If so, it is the only verbal quotation from the Gospels in St Paul's writings. Or is it possible that the first two words of the Paternoster were pronounced, in the first age of the Church, bilingually, just as we still talk Greek and then translate it into Latin when we recite the Reproaches on Good Friday? Nobody can tell you. But when St Paul uses little touches like that, one